Football
SKILLS OF THE GAME

Jim Kelman

HODDER
Wayland

Other titles in the series:
Rules of the Game
Players and Tactics
Teamwork!

For more information on this series and
other Hodder Wayland titles,
go to www.hodderwayland.co.uk

Produced for Wayland
Publishers Limited by
Thunderbolt Partnership
Editors: Janet de Saulles
Paula Field
Designer: Eljay Yidirim
Photography: Steve Gorton
Artwork: Phillp Morrision

First published by
Wayland Publishers Limited
This edition published in 2006
by Hodder Wayland, an imprint
of Hodder Children's Books
338 Euston Road, London
NW1 3BH

British Library Cataloguing in
Publication Data
Kelman, Jim
Skills of the Game. - (Soccer)
1. Soccer - Juvenile literature
1.Title 796 . 3' 34
ISBN-10: 0750249471
ISBN-13: 9780750249478

Printed in China

Foreword from Sir Clive Woodward:
For all young children who take part in the game
of football, these books will give an excellent insight
into the techniques and understanding that will help
them to become more knowledgeable and improve
their playing skills.

Contents

Introduction

Football is played by two teams and many people think it is the finest 'invasion' game in the world. It has one main aim – each team must move the ball into the other team's end of the pitch and score in their goal.

Attacking

In the first half of this book, you will learn how to 'attack' – you will see how important it is to keep the ball in your possession! By running with the ball, by dribbling, turning, controlling, passing, and then shooting or heading, your team will try to score.

▲ Once you have got the ball, and there is space in front of you, kick the ball firmly forward and run with it.

▶ The defenders from a local South African club fight for possession of the ball as the opposition attacker races through towards the goal.

Defending

The second half of this book shows you what to do when the other team have the ball. Now you must 'defend'. This means you must try to stop the other team from scoring.

Enjoy the game!

Football is all about having fun. So remember, whether you are just playing with a group of friends, or whether you are taking part in an important match, enjoy the game!

Attacking play

When your team is on the attack, you must keep the ball in your possession and try to score a goal.

DRIBBLING

Dribbling is running with the ball close to your feet, pushing it forwards with controlled, soft taps. It allows you to take the ball towards a defender, tricking the player with your body in order to get past. It takes practice and quick feet to be good at dribbling.

▼ The player has moved his weight to his left foot to touch the ball away with his right foot. Dribbling is all about change of pace and direction.

▲ Play the ball from one foot to the other when you dribble.

Two dribbling tricks

⚽ When your opponent moves one way, lean and push the ball in the opposite direction (scissors).

⚽ When a defender stands in front of you, play the ball through his or her legs (nutmeg).

GREAT DRIBBLERS USE **BOTH** FEET!

◀ The scissors
1. Get ready to kick the ball with the inside of one foot.
2. Fake a movement over the ball to unbalance your opponent.
3. Now lean and take the ball in the opposite direction.

COACH'S NOTES
Practise touching the ball with both feet while skipping from foot to foot.

▲ The nutmeg
1. Pretend to take the ball across your opponent.
2. Wait until the defender has his feet apart.
3. Now push the ball through his legs.

TURNING

When defenders are close to you, you may have to turn away from them. This will give you time to work out how to keep the ball. Here are some basic turns to get you away from the defender, while keeping the ball.

▲ Inside foot
1. The defender is getting too close.
2. Try turning using the inside of the foot nearest to the defender and move away.

◀ Outside foot
1. The defender is again too close.
2. Try turning using the outside of the foot furthest from the defender.

▶ The stop turn
1. Use the sole of your boot to stop the ball.
2. Step over it.
3. Quickly turn around to face the ball.

▶ The drag back

1. Pretend to kick the ball, then put your foot on top of it.
2. Drag the ball back and spin it, using the outside of the same foot.

▲ The Cruyff turn

1. Pretend to kick the ball.
2. Put your foot in front it.
3. Now drag the ball back through your legs, turning away from the defender.

▶ The step-over turn

1. Step over the ball.
2. Pretend to continue the run forward.
3. Spin the back foot around keeping your weight on the front foot.
4. Go back the way you came pushing the ball with the outside of the front foot.

PASSING THE BALL

The best time to pass the ball is when you are under pressure from one or more defenders, and you see a team mate in a much better position.

Passing the ball

Trick defenders by making your body look as though you're going to pass the ball one way, but then kick it another. Or pretend to pass with the inside of your foot, then play the ball with the outside of your foot.

COACH'S NOTES

Pretend to pass to a team mate. When your marker moves to block the pass, quickly run past him.

◀ Keep the ball at ground level using the inside of your foot.

Outside of foot

Inside of foot

◀ Practise moving the ball around using different parts of your feet. This will help you have more control over the ball.

Receiving the ball

When the ball is passed to you, try to remember these tips.

⚽ Balance on the front of your feet and concentrate on the ball.

⚽ Move into the path of the ball.

⚽ Decide which part of your feet or body you are going to use to stop and control the ball.

⚽ If you use your feet, cushion the ball. That is, move your foot back as the ball hits it. This stops the ball from bouncing off.

▲ Get ready to receive the ball, by getting into a balanced position with your weight on the front part of your feet.

11

HEADING THE BALL

Outfield players (which is all players on the pitch except the goalkeeper) use their feet and body to control the ball. Only goalkeepers can use their hands. But everybody on the pitch is allowed to use their head.

▶ To stop attackers getting the ball, head the ball upwards. Call out your name so your team mates keep out of your way.

▲ Heading down
Hit the top part of the ball with your forehead. Jump high to head the ball low.

◀ Heading up
Hit the bottom of the ball with your forehead. Add power by using your legs and back.

▶ Attacking headers

Heading the ball down and into the corners of the goal is a good way of beating the goalkeeper.

▲ Defensive headers

You need courage for these. While the ball is in the air and coming towards you, move quickly to get to the ball first and head the ball clear or to a team mate.

ONLY USE YOUR **FOREHEAD** WHEN YOU HEAD THE BALL

▲ Diving headers

If the ball reaches you below waist height, dive and head the ball. Keep your arms out in front to cushion your landing.

SCORING

Not all attacking moves will end in a goal, but to increase your chances of scoring there are some golden rules to remember: try to keep the ball low; aim for the far corner of the goal; and always vary the type of shot you make. You could chip the ball, swerve it, head it or volley it to score a goal.

▲ You will always be under pressure to go for a goal quickly. In this Premiership match the striker has aimed a powerful but controlled shot for the top corner of the net just out of the goalkeeper's reach.

Accuracy, not power

The accuracy of your shot is more important than power. Although hard shots are difficult for goalkeepers to save, you are very likely to put the ball high or wide.

KICK
AGAINST YOUR
LACES
TO GET
POWERFUL
SHOTS.

Shooting tips

▶ Chip the ball

Put your toes under the ball, point your foot down and kick the ball with a stabbing action. This sends the ball high into the air with a backward spin, making it difficult for the goalkeeper to stop it.

▼ Swerve the ball

Striking the ball hard off centre will cause the ball to curl around the goalkeeper.

▶ Volley the ball

If you don't have time to control the ball before kicking it, try a volley. This means striking the ball while it is still in mid air.

Defensive play

When the other team have the ball you must 'defend'. This means you must challenge the other team and try to get the ball back so that you can score.

CHALLENGING

If you are the person nearest to the player with the ball, move quickly and get as close to the ball as possible.

The defending position
Balance your weight on the front part of your feet, keeping your knees slightly bent. One foot should be in a forward position.

► This shows a good defending position. The defender (right) is balanced and keeping his eye on the ball.

▲ A good defending position allows you to block your opponent's pass or shot at goal.

Staying on your feet

Once you are in position near the ball, be patient and watch the ball. Do not lunge for it – you will end up flat on your back!

▼ Make sure you stay on your feet. If you fall over the attacker will move past you towards your goal.

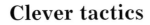

Clever tactics

A good tactic is to pretend to rush in. Stay balanced and move your upper body towards your opponent. He or she may move with the ball, perhaps showing too much of it. Steal the ball now and attack your opponent's goal.

▲ **Steal the ball**
1. Get in close and try to unsettle him or her.
2. Steal the ball.

COACH'S NOTES
If the pitch is wet and slippery, it will be more difficult to defend well.

17

SUPPORTING YOUR TEAM MATES

When one of your team is putting pressure on an opponent (letting them know they are under close watch) ask yourself how you can help.

Supporting Tactics

▲ Always support your team mate. Never leave him alone to mark the attacker with the ball.

Let your team mate know you are in a good supporting position by calling out your name.

If the opponent gets past your team mate, you should be ready to pressure him or her yourself.

While your team mate challenges his or her opponent, the other team members should move to cover any other attackers who are free.

COACH'S NOTES

Good defenders try to cover all the attackers who are likely to receive a pass.

▲ Making a challenge

Defender (1) failed to win the ball from the attacker, but defender (2) is ready to make a challenge.

▲ Pressure, support, cover

Player (1) is challenging player (2). His team mates (3 and 5) are supporting him by covering player (4). If player (1) fails to win the challenge and the ball is passed to player (4), then players (3) and (5) can challenge themselves.

INTERCEPTING AND RECOVERY

Intercepting means getting to the ball before your opponent receives it from a team mate.

Marking

This is where you stay just behind an opponent and are ready to tackle or steal the ball if it is passed to him.

The defending triangle

Make sure you can see both the opponent who is about to pass the ball and the opponent you are marking. These are the first two points in a defending triangle. You are the third point.

ALWAYS BE READY TO CHALLENGE OR STEAL THE BALL

▲ **A defending triangle**
Player (1) forms a defending triangle by moving into a position where he can see the ball and the player (2) he is marking.

Getting back in position

If you go forward in an attempt to score, you will sometimes lose the ball and get left behind. You need to get back quickly to help your team mates defend. This is called a recovery run.

COACH'S NOTES
Remember, the time it takes you to get back into a defensive position is time that your team is playing without you.

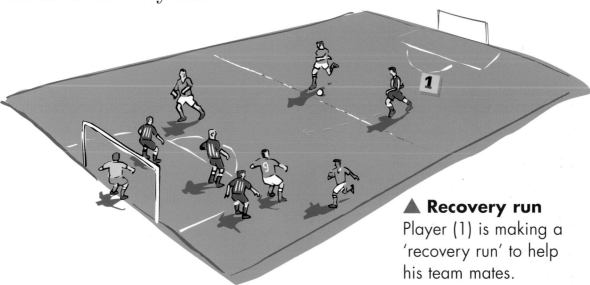

▲ **Recovery run**
Player (1) is making a 'recovery run' to help his team mates.

Recovery run tactics

⚽ Run towards the middle of your own goal.

⚽ Once you are level with an opponent you can relax!

⚽ If that opponent is the one with the ball, you must pressure him to win the ball back again.

PREVENTING TURNING

Many goals are scored by players who get a pass and then turn with the ball. To stop this dangerous move, stay alert and be ready to defend so that you will see the ball being passed to the player you are marking.

EVERYONE DEFENDS IF THEIR TEAM DOESN'T HAVE THE BALL

Putting on the pressure

When your opponent receives the ball, putting on pressure by getting close will encourage him to make a mistake.

▲ To prevent your opponent from turning, run to a position just behind him, making sure you can see the ball.

Being turned

Don't rush in too quickly or get too close to your opponent. He can spin around you with the ball. This is called being turned.

◀ If you move in too quickly and get too close then you will be turned by the attacker.

How to prevent turning

If you are nicely balanced with one foot forward, and you can see the ball, you are in a good defending position. Try and be patient. The player with the ball will know you are there and feel under pressure. When the right moment comes, move in and steal the ball.

▼ This defender is in a good balanced defending position to prevent his opponent from turning.

STOPPING FORWARD PLAY

If the player you are moving towards has already turned with the ball, you must try to stop the ball being played forward.

A curving run

Player (1) has beaten his challenger and is ready to pass the ball to his team mate (2). But defender (3) is making a curving run into his opponent's line of vision, which will make it difficult for him to pass the ball forward.

Try these tactics:

⚽ Check where you think the ball is to be played.

⚽ Don't allow your opponent to move past you because you have rushed in too close or even fallen down.

⚽ Be patient – get close and stand in the defending position, keeping one foot forward.

⚽ Pretend to tackle, then steal the ball from your opponent instead.

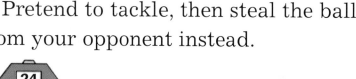

24

Denying space

The 'defending triangle' (p.20) is a good position for single players and for the whole team to use. When the team forms defending triangles, it is difficult for the opposition to pass the ball through them.

ALWAYS BLOCK SPACE THROUGH THE MIDDLE OF THE PITCH

◀ Winning the ball back

In this diagram, the (X) players have blocked the space through the middle of the pitch. The only way for the (O) team to pass the ball is either around the outside of the (X) team, or by way of a long pass through the air. Both of these passes give the (X) team a greater chance of intercepting and winning the ball back.

COACH'S NOTES

When you lose possession of the ball, always deny your opponents the space to move or pass the ball into.

25

After the ball is won

Once you have won possession of the ball, your team must spread out. The front players must position themselves further up the pitch. This makes it easier for your team to pass the ball forward.

▲ The two attackers (blue) have spread out, leaving one defender to mark them both – this tactic makes it much more difficult for defenders to make successful tackles.

▶ A passing angle

If your team mate (1) is unable to pass the ball forward because a defender (2) is in the way, move to a position (X) where you can see the ball easily to create a 'passing angle.'

Supporting from behind the ball

When your team's front players are positioned up the pitch, they can give support from in front of the ball. It is also important, however, to give support from behind the ball.

▼ Playing wide

If you see that your team mate (1) is being pressured by defenders in midfield, run out to the wing where he or she can pass the ball to you.

Using the whole pitch

When your team has possession of the ball, all your players should position themselves so that they can see the ball and the rest of the pitch. If your goalkeeper or defenders have possession, then it is important for your wide players to get as close to the touchline as possible.

COACH'S NOTES
When you play wide, play so wide that you are almost off the pitch!

27

CREATING SPACE

Your team can make space by spreading out and moving to make passing angles. But it is important that you create space for yourself.

Faking and dodging

It takes quite a lot of skill to lose your opponent! But you can do this by faking and dodging. To dodge your opponent, pretend to move away. He or she will follow you. Then you must come back towards the ball into the space you have created.

 Dodging

1. Pretend to move away from your opponent. He will follow you.
2. Run back into the space you have made.
3. Be ready to receive the ball from your team mate.

Timing your run

Once your team have spread out, there will be lots of space to run into. Always time your run into the space so that you arrive at the same time as the ball. If you arrive before the ball, you will block the space and have to wait around for the ball.

GOOD PLAYERS **RUN, FAKE AND DODGE** EVEN WHEN THEY HAVE NOT GOT THE BALL!

COACH'S NOTES
Time your run into the space between defenders so that the ball can be played to you.

▲ Perfect timing
In the diagram, player (1) has timed his run perfectly so that he can get to the ball before the defenders and get a clear shot on goal.

Glossary

Attacking header
Heading the ball into the corners of the goal.

Being balanced Standing with your legs comfortably apart and with your knees bent. Your weight should be placed on the front part of your feet.

Chipping the ball
Kicking the ball so that it goes up in the air and comes steeply back down to the ground.

Creating space When a team spreads out and creates passing angles.

Cruyff turn A type of turn where you pretend to kick, put your foot in front of the ball and drag it back through your legs, turning away from the defender.

Cushioning the ball
Stopping the ball bouncing off your foot when it is passed to you by moving your foot back as the ball hits it.

Defending triangle
When you can see both the opponent who is about to pass the ball and the opponent you are marking. You form the third 'point' of this triangle.

Defensive header
Heading the ball when it is in the air and coming towards you.

Denying space When the whole team get into defensive triangles, making it difficult for the opposition to pass the ball.

Diving header Diving downwards to head the ball if it reaches you below waist height.

Drag back A type of turn where you pretend to kick the ball, put your foot on top of it, drag it back and spin it, using the outside of the same foot.

Dribbling Running with the ball close to your feet, and pushing it forwards with quick, sharp kicks.

Faking and dodging
Pretending to move or kick the ball.

Heading Passing the ball by hitting it with your forehead.

Nutmeg Dribbling trick where you push the ball through your opponent's legs.

Outfield player All players on the field except the goalkeepers.

Passing angle Being in a position where you can see the ball easily so that it can be passed to you.

Passing the ball Moving the ball from one team member to another.

Pressuring Letting the player you are marking know they are under close watch.

Recovery run Running back to your place on the pitch after going forward in an attempt to score.

Scissors movement A dribbling trick where you move your feet across the ball one way, but then take the ball in another direction.

Scoring Sending the ball into goal.

Stealing the ball
Regaining possession of the ball.

Step-over turn Stepping over the ball, spinning around, and going back the way you came.

Stop turn Stopping the ball with the sole of your boot, jumping over it, then quickly turning around to face the ball.

Support Being near to another member of your team and being ready to help.

Swerve Curling the ball around the goalkeeper by striking it hard off centre.

Tactics Ways of keeping or getting the ball.

Turning Moving away from a defender.

Further Information

Football Associations

English F.A., 25 Soho Square, London W1D 4FA
www.thefa.com

Scottish F.A., Hampden Park, Glasgow G42 9AY
www.scottishfa.co.uk

F.A. of Wales, Plymouth Chambers, 3 Westgate Street, Cardiff CF10 1DP
www.fawtrust.org.uk

Irish F.A. (Northern Ireland), 20 Windsor Avenue, Belfast BT9 6EG
www.irishfa.com

F.A. of Ireland (Republic of Ireland), 80 Merreon Square, Dubin 2
www.fai.ie

Books

Defensive Soccer Tactics by Jens Bangbo and Berger Pietersen
(Human Kinetics Europe, 2001)
SAQ Soccer: Speed, Agility and Quickness for Soccer by
Alan Pearson (A&C Black, 2001)
The Football Association Coaching Book of Soccer Tactics and Skills by
Charles Hughes (Queen Anne Press, 1994)
The Practices and Training Sessions of the World's Top Teams and Coaches
by Mike Saif (Reedswain Incorporated, 2000)
Youth Soccer Drills by Jim Garland (Human Kinetics Europe, 2003)

WEBSITE DISCLAIMER:
The website addresses (URLs) included in this book were valid at
the time of going to press. However, because of the nature of the
Internet, it is possible that some addresses may have changed, or
sites may have changed or closed down since publication. While
the authors and Publisher regret any inconvenience this may
cause readers, no responsibility for any such changes can be
accepted by either the authors or the Publisher.

ACKNOWLEDGEMENTS
We would like to thank the following people for their help
with this book: The Football Association, Nikki Kelman,
Mike Fowles and the boys and girls of Wynchcombe Junior
Schol, Hendon F.C.

PICTURE CREDITS:
P5 Allsport, P14 t Allsport.

Index